Staying Well:
Strategies for Corrections Staff

3rd Edition

Caterina G. Spinaris, Ph.D.

Florence, Colorado

Staying Well: Strategies for Corrections Staff, 3rd Edition
By Caterina G. Spinaris

Mission of Desert Waters Correctional Outreach
"To promote the occupational, personal and family
well-being of the corrections workforce
through the provision of evidence-informed
resources, solutions, and support."

Cover design by Mary Dilley.

Published by Desert Waters Correctional Outreach (DWCO).
Printed in the U.S.A. by Our Daily Bread Ministries,
Grand Rapids, MI.

ISBN: 978-1-7923-0518-4   (paper)

This publication may be ordered from:
Desert Waters Correctional Outreach
http://desertwaters.com
719-784-4727

DWCO, P.O. Box 355, Florence, CO 81226-0355

TABLE OF CONTENTS

DEDICATION

This book is dedicated to all the
corrections professionals and their families
that I treated, trained and talked with
informally since the year 2000. You trusted me
with your innermost experiences and truths –
with your victories and also with your struggles.
Thanks to your courage, openness, and desire
to move forward – and to move the profession
forward – **you became my teachers**.
And that is why we can now offer this book.

Caterina G. Spinaris

ENDORSEMENTS

"I personally believe that this book will give corrections officers **hope**. It will also **equip them with the tools necessary to be effective at their job** while dealing with the stress of the workplace."

~Denny Kaemingk, *Cabinet Secretary,*
South Dakota Department of Corrections (Retired)

"The AOCE General Membership voted to purchase 1,000 copies of the Staying Well book. We then mailed the book to each individual staff member's home, so they and their families could read it. I have received **great feedback** from both our Officers and Non-Custody staff. **It has helped many of them in starting the process of healing.** If they don't know what's happening with them or how to fix it, they will remain stagnant or falter. The book is worth the money even if it only helps one staff member. Here in Oregon, **it has helped MANY and will continue to help many more for YEARS to come.**"

~Sgt. Michael Van Patten, *President,*
Association of Oregon Corrections Employees

"The information in this booklet should be shared in every academy and training that occurs in local, state, and federal prisons and jails. It is **accurate, concise, insightful, and comes from years of information gathering.**"

~T.C. Brown, *Corrections Professional*

"Correctional workers are the most misunderstood of all law enforcement professionals. This booklet addresses some of the issues faced by correctional professionals, and offers techniques and skills to ensure that the correctional worker career is enjoyed and that stresses of the job are mitigated. This is **an excellent resource for anyone working in corrections, their family members, or anyone providing assistance to a correctional professional.** It is written in understandable language and gives real examples of issues faced."

~Dr. Manuel A. Cordero, *former Assistant to the Bureau of Prisons Chief of Chaplains*

FOREWORD

Dear Correctional Worker:

When is the last time someone asked you how you were doing, and you answered honestly?

When is the last time that you even thought about how you are doing, honestly?

For most of us, these times may be hard to recall. I urge you now to set aside a few moments to take an inventory of your health, what is important to you in life, and what the future holds. I urge you to use this book to guide you through a process that will help with this inventory.

While some of the information in this book may be hard to hear and even harder to admit, it needs to be said, and it needs to be shared. This book is meant to be shared. Share it with your significant other, share it with your co-workers, and anyone else in your life who matters to you. Your health and the health of your co-workers are at stake.

Corrections workers are experts at building walls, keeping people and feelings out. It is time to let these walls down and let in some positive help. This book provides some guidance on how to do just that—let in the positive and improve your life.

This book will also help you prepare and persevere for your retirement years. You must take steps now to ensure that there is something left of you when your corrections agency is through with you.

Make that "something left" something vital and significant.

The work each of you do is too important, and must be done with utmost precision.

However, the work must not be allowed to consume you!

~Susan Jones, Ph.D.
Colorado Department of Corrections (Retired)

"I AM A CORRECTIONAL PROFESSIONAL"
By Brent Parker

I am a PERSON
I am young and old, tall and short, man and woman; and I am of all faiths
I am a father, mother, brother, and sister; I am a son and a daughter, and I am a single parent
I am from all parts of this great country and I am a citizen of my community
I wear a uniform or I don't
I maintain the highest standards, and I represent my agency
I see things that hurt my soul and damage my spirit, but I maintain hope
I lead by example, and I am a good and decent human being
I have a family of loved ones at home and a family of partners at work
I feel, I care, I rejoice, I am a PERSON

I am a WORKER
I am well-trained and part of a good team
I work with men, women, and youthful offenders
I work with many cultures, races, and faiths
I work evenings, nights, and weekends, holidays and birthdays

I stand at a post, man a tower, carry a gun
I transport, search, and move offenders
I train staff, write policy, maintain standards, and
keep safety high
I supervise good people and hold my partners
accountable
I maintain buildings, locks, vehicles, radios,
phones, computers, fences, and weapons
I work behind the scenes in cramped offices to
make sure the ship keeps running smoothly
I am sometimes verbally and physically abused,
yet I maintain my professionalism
I accept that my work is stressful; yet I maintain
my honor, I am a **WORKER**

I am a PROVIDER
I provide good food, clean clothes, and protection
I provide education, vocation, work skills, and
opportunity
I provide GED, reading, writing, and math classes,
and recreation
I provide medical, dental, and vision care
I provide hospice care and dignity
I provide reentry opportunities, legal access, and
religious programs
I provide hope
I provide mental health, substance abuse, and

anger treatment

I provide a bed, a roof, warmth, and food, I am a
PROVIDER

I PROTECT

I keep offenders safe while sleeping, working,
resting, and playing

I supervise parolees and offenders in community
corrections and ISPs

I provide suicide watch to protect people from
themselves

I control contraband and maintain facility and
public safety

I control access. I keep offenders in and others out

I protect offenders, partners, visitors, and
volunteers from harm

I protect the public, 24 hours a day, 365 days a
year—all day, every day

I PROTECT Them, Us, and YOU

I do what I do because I serve my community, my
agency, my state, and my country.

I am a Person, a Worker, a Provider, and a
Protector.

I am not a guard;

I am your Corrections Professional.

CHAPTER 1
THE TOLL OF THE JOB

As a corrections professional, you operate in work environments that are chronically and routinely taxing. You are ever-vigilant. You multi-task, often under time pressure, in the presence of potential or actual danger and/or health crises, and in the midst of a seemingly incessant barrage of human demands and needs—while also having to discern whether requests or behaviors are genuine or not. You courageously run towards situations most people would run away from. At a moment's notice, you put your "people" skills to work to take control of volatile situations and to de-escalate conflict. You problem-solve on your feet, sometimes in the midst of chaotic situations. You exercise remarkable patience and self-control in the face of repeated provocations. You protect lives. You save lives. You shape lives, perhaps for generations to come. You keep offenders and staff in corrections facilities and community-based offices safe. Ultimately, you help keep whole towns and cities safe. YOU MAKE IT HAPPEN.

And, not surprisingly, there is a price you pay as you continue to absorb the shock of jarring aspects of your job. This price may involve your physical health due to wear-and-tear effects on your body. Or the job may impact you at a deeper level. A corrections officer summed it up in these words: "What I come across at work wounds my soul." Was he unique in his experience? Regrettably, my history of training and treating corrections staff since the year 2000 tells me that his experience is far from unusual. This corrections officer simply put into words what many corrections professionals go through, but do not often talk about.

Examples of the negative fallout of the job on individual staff include lowered job performance, professional misconduct, strained or broken relationships, physical illnesses, psychological disorders, substance abuse, and even suicide. At the organizational level negative consequences include unhealthy workplace cultures, low staff morale, poor teamwork, high sick leave rates, high short-term disability rates, and high staff turnover.

Three main types of stressors bombard corrections personnel regularly and often, sometimes simultaneously or in close succession. These three categories are operational stressors, organizational stressors, and traumatic stressors.

Operational stressors refer to occupational challenges that arise as part of routine, day-to-day operations. They can include staffing numbers, shift work, offender management issues, mandatory overtime, job assignments, equipment and supplies availability and condition, physical environmental conditions, some training issues, professional role ambiguity or conflict (security vs. helping), and some policies and procedures.

Organizational stressors refer to interpersonal issues and aspects of staff management. They may stem from leadership philosophies; managerial or supervisory styles; workplace culture ideologies; pay; benefits; procedures for performance evaluation, internal investigations or discipline; and promotion practices, among others. Additionally, organizational stressors may result from the general public's misperceptions about the profession, a predominantly negative public image, and political scrutiny.

Traumatic stressors refer to exposure to incidents of death, injury, or violence (including sexual violence). Such incidents may be experienced directly, when staff members are themselves assaulted. Or they may be witnessed directly in real time, such as when staff respond to an incident. Or staff may be exposed to traumatic stressors indirectly, such as when they read or hear about such events, or view them electronically at a later time. Threats of violence—"what could happen," and "near misses"— "what could have happened" are also types of indirect traumatic exposure.

Repeated exposure to these three types of occupational stressors, coupled with the need for continual watchfulness and anticipation of others' "next move," is more often than not the norm in corrections work. A corrections officer likened the essence of his job to playing a high-stakes game of chess daily, where a wrong move could result in conflict, investigations, disciplinary measures, legal ramifications, injuries, and even death. And coming back to continue the next day. And then the day after that. For twenty to thirty years.

Consequently, as time goes on, staff might end up getting wound up more and more tightly. And when they get off work, they may find it increasingly hard to relax and engage with people outside of corrections in healthy ways. They discover that the advice, "Don't take work home," or "Leave it at the gate" is easier said than done.

This booklet was written to describe how work experiences can shape corrections staff negatively. It was also written to suggest ways for staff to overcome or avoid these adverse effects, growing positively instead as people and as professionals, with healthy family lives and fulfilling careers.

Ultimately, this booklet was written to come alongside you, and to let you know that we "see" you and care about you.

The booklet's contents apply to prison and jail employees—such as security/custody of all ranks, education, religious services, medical, mental health, administrative, Information Technology, clerical, and maintenance staff. It also applies to probation and/or parole agents, supervisors, support and administrative staff at community corrections offices and at work-release centers. Lastly, it applies to staff working with justice-involved juveniles in various capacities and settings.

The following stories illustrate some of the struggles experienced by corrections personnel. Details were altered to render staff unidentifiable. These are *not* "problem children." On the contrary, they are hardworking, seasoned, and conscientious employees. When you come across staff like them, you would never guess their struggles. They wear their "I'm good!" mask, acting like nothing bothers them. Are they rare? Unfortunately, not.

"I've been horribly short-tempered with my family lately. Four months ago I was viciously assaulted

by two offenders. Since then I prefer to stay away from everybody. I keep replaying the incident in my mind, and having nightmares about it. In the morning I wake up feeling exhausted. Lately, I started drinking before going to bed. It helps me fall asleep. I don't like doing that, but I can't see myself going to a shrink. I did go to my family doctor though, because I started having headaches that wouldn't quit. Now I'm on meds for high blood pressure."

~ *Corrections Officer*

"In social situations I get terribly tense. I feel like I'm in danger, and that I need to get out or push people away, even when I know there is no danger. I make excuses to avoid social events unless I know that only a handful of people will be there. When I'm given a table at a restaurant (or even have to sit in a room with other people), if I can't put my back up against a wall, I leave. I hate not being able to enjoy social situations, and I hate putting my wife through this. Recently I was diagnosed with acid reflux."

~ *Corrections Officer*

"At work I go non-stop. Some of the health problems I've seen are unbelievable. And I'm caught between the officers and offenders. The officers mistrust me, because they think I give offenders all the 'candy' they want. And the offenders yell at me

when I say 'No.' The other day an offender went off on me. He was so close, I could feel his spit hitting my face. I fear for my safety."
~Correctional Nurse

"I can't seem to get along with anyone anymore. The only people I want to be close to are my husband and my daughter, and they don't want to be close to me because I am miserable all the time. Some days I just can't stand my job anymore, but then I go back. Perhaps I'm trying to prove something. Or I'm addicted to my paycheck. After a couple of incidents with gangbangers, I've become nervous about going in. And we have some staff who make each other's lives hell. I don't know who's harder to take—the offenders or the staff. When I really think about it though, it's the staff that's the worst. With offenders I know what to expect. But with coworkers, I never know what they're going to pull. To keep away from both, I've switched to nights. Now with all the sodas I drink to stay awake, my size keeps increasing.
~ Corrections Officer

"As a Probation/Parole Officer I deal with addicts, burglars, gang-bangers, and murderers—to name a few. They blame everybody else for their problems. My job role is endless, and the list of my duties keeps growing (but my pay does not). I am the social worker, attorney (I represent the State's case),

cop, counselor, victim advocate, cheerleader, debt collector, paper pusher, community liaison, parent, therapist, coach. I am the one who gets blamed whenever anything goes wrong. I get yelled at by clients, by their families, by victims, by law enforcement, by attorneys, by judges, by treatment professionals, by supervisors. Lately I've started looking for alternative employment."
~ *Probation & Parole Officer*

"When I applied for the job I was sold. I really wanted to help troubled kids stay away from drugs and gangs. But doing this work is changing me more than it's changing them. The kids' stories haunt me. What was done to them, and what they did to others and to animals. Yes, some do get better, but many of them keep going back to the wrong people, getting beat up or raped over and over. Or they get arrested for new crimes. Most of the time now I'm irritable, exhausted, and gloomy. I know I wasn't like that before starting this profession. I used to enjoy hanging out with friends and meeting new people. Now I just don't like people anymore. When I'm off work, I mostly want to be left alone. Some days I think I should quit and find a 'normal' job."
~ *Juvenile Counselor*

"The job is getting to me. I feel like I'm just getting a paycheck and not making any difference.

When I get home after work, I treat my two boys
like offenders, screaming at them if they make any
noise, and expecting them to do as I say immedi-
ately. They don't deserve that kind of treatment.
My wife is fed up with me being mad all the time.
If she tries to argue with me about anything, I
blow up. I'm ashamed of my behavior, and I don't
like living like this, but I don't know how to snap
out of it. Lately I haven't been able to shake the
anxiety and depression I feel, even while I'm on
medication. And I keep gaining weight."
~ *Correctional Teacher*

These stories illustrate how lack of use of effective coping strategies and resources can undermine
staff's quality of life, and collectively undercut organizational health and functioning.

Systematic and data-driven efforts are essential to
counter the toll of corrections work, and to promote
professional excellence and fulfillment. Solutions require both top-down (organizational) and bottom-up
(individual) efforts. Organizations need to acknowledge and, whenever possible, lessen occupational
stressors; teach staff evidence-based resilience and
wellness skills; and provide relevant, affordable,
and sufficient helping resources. And individual employees need to do their part—diligently apply the
wellness and resilience skills they are taught, and use
available resources.

Increasingly more corrections agencies are acknowledging the impact of the job on corrections employees, and offer more, and more specialized, resources and services to promote staff wellness. This is great progress—much more of which is needed.

Reflection

What came to mind as you read the staff stories?

CHAPTER 2
CORRECTIONS FATIGUE

"Corrections Fatigue" is a term I coined in the year 2000 to describe the cumulative negative effects of occupational stressors on corrections staff.

Engineers speak of metal fatigue. A perfectly good piece of metal, if repeatedly stressed, eventually becomes pliable, weaker, and "fatigued." Metal fatigue can happen to even the strongest of stock, and the changes that occur go all the way down to the molecular level. When metal becomes sufficiently "fatigued," even steel bridges collapse and airplane wings break off.

Similarly, corrections staff—no matter how tough they are—can gradually become "fatigued" as they try to adapt to ongoing job challenges. Fatigue-related changes are the cumulative outcome of repeated exposures to correctional stressors. They affect staff's personality, health and functioning, and their core beliefs and ideology. (The term "ideology" refers to a system of beliefs or ideals held by individuals or groups.) These changes constitute what I call "Corrections Fatigue."

This construct is based on the work of psychologists Lisa McCann, Laurie Anne Pearlman and Karen Saakvitne, who described changes in individuals following exposure to traumatic stressors.[1,2]

Given the multitude of stressors to which corrections staff are exposed during the course of their careers, Corrections Fatigue is an unavoidable occupational hazard. Negative changes may be hardly detectable at first. If not countered with effective strategies, however, they continue to add up, eventually becoming ingrained, "hard-wired," and emotionally distressing.

Corrections Fatigue is not a clinical diagnosis or disorder. Rather, it is an "umbrella" term that describes the combined and cumulative effects of occupational stressors on corrections staff.

Signs of Corrections Fatigue manifest on a continuum of severity. At any one point in time, staff may manifest no signs, minor signs, moderate, severe, or extreme signs. When moderate or more severe signs exist, staff members may be diagnosed as suffering from physical or psychological health conditions.

If the number of affected staff in a workforce is sufficiently high, the entire culture exhibits signs of Corrections Fatigue.

Sounds grim, doesn't it? There is good news, though: Corrections Fatigue CAN be dealt with, countered, and even be prevented! Solutions do exist!

The rest of this chapter discusses Correction Fatigue contributors, consequences, and phases of professional change in relation to Corrections Fatigue.

FACTORS THAT CONTRIBUTE TO CORRECTIONS FATIGUE

Below are some work-related factors which can contribute to Corrections Fatigue. Additional ones can be identified, depending on the workplace culture.

1. **Nature of the job.** Corrections work is inherently adversarial. Offenders, whether in facilities or in the community, may (naturally) resent restrictions on their freedoms, viewing corrections staff as "the enemy." Additionally, security/custody work tends to be highly structured and monotonous. When an emergency occurs, however, staff are instantly transformed to warriors. The intensity of the stress response taxes the staff's bodies, even though at the time it may feel exhilarating. As for probation/parole agents, their work tends to be ever changing, unpredictable, and potentially dangerous as they supervise clients during home visits or office appointments.

2. **Role ambiguity or conflict.** Corrections professionals are required to engage offenders on two levels: rule enforcement—custody and control, maintaining safety and security; and rehabilitation—care and treatment, engaging offenders in pro-social activities, and preparing them for re-entry into society. Staff must confront offender insubordination, and administer consequences accordingly. They are also expected to be positive role models, listen, motivate, help, and support. These two requirements of "law enforcer" and "helper" may be experienced by staff as hard to juggle, because they require switching their mindset, interaction styles, and operating modes depending on circumstances.

3. **Nature of the offenders.** Offenders may be anti-social, violent, gang-affiliated, and/or drug-addicted, with histories of psychological trauma, and neurological disorders—such as learning disabilities. Mentally ill offenders may be highly unpredictable, acting erratically and violently towards themselves or others.

4. **Nature of the organization.** Given the paramilitary structure of corrections, frontline staff may come to believe that administrators regard them as "warm bodies," not valued persons. This is especially the case when the chain of

command does not encourage two-way communications or input from lower ranks to higher ones. Moreover, the mere size of large agencies, and possibly strained labor relations, can contribute to staff experiencing alienation from their leadership, viewing them as unsupportive or adversarial. Non-security staff may feel even less esteemed by both administrators and security/custody staff.

5. **Workplace culture.** Related to the nature of the organization is the corrections workplace culture, which is one of toughness, where empathy and kindness are regarded as liabilities likely to cause staff to be exploited. In such cultures, emotional struggles, seeking help, having doubts, or making mistakes, are regarded as unacceptable signs of weakness. Showing compassion for offenders is also frowned upon, as it is viewed as the first step towards crossing professional boundaries. The predominant mindset is "us against them."

6. **Negative workplace environment.** Prevailing emotional undercurrents of corrections environments are fear, anger, hate, sadness, and despair. These are coupled with the scarcity of tenderness and compassion. Austere surroundings, lack of natural beauty, and harsh physical conditions—such as extreme temperatures, lack of cleanli-

ness, offender overcrowding, and noise—add to the bleakness of the work environment. And some employees may taunt, intimidate, threaten, or otherwise abuse others, or act deceitfully and even criminally. The end result of such behaviors is a workplace where staff mistrust and/or fear coworkers, or clash with them, often dreading going to work.

7. **Sexual harassment.** Staff may be sexually harassed by coworkers through comments or coercion for sexual involvement. Targeted staff may be threatened with retaliation if they complain or if they do not comply with sexual requests. Women staff in particular may also be exposed to sexual harassment by offenders through comments or sexual behaviors. On the flip side, staff falsely accused of sexually inappropriate behaviors towards offenders or staff undergo lengthy and highly stressful investigations. And they may still be viewed as perpetrators, even after being cleared.

8. **Witnessing policy violations.** In the course of their work, staff may encounter "bad apples," employees who grievously violate departmental policies. Observing such behavior is highly stressful to coworkers. This is especially so for new or low-ranking staff,

particularly if they are alone in their observations, or if they are aware that the "code of silence" is in operation. Staff know that they must report violations, yet they may fear being retaliated against by coworkers.

9. **Work overload.** Multi-tasking, increased staff duties due to short-staffing, and mandatory overtime contribute to physical and mental exhaustion that feeds Corrections Fatigue. This frequently occurs in the context of sleep deprivation due to shift work. The work load gets even heavier when necessary equipment is non-existent or unreliable due to malfunctioning.

10. **Exposure to traumatic material.** Corrections staff are indirectly exposed to traumatic material frequently. They also witness life-threatening events, and endure physical assaults and threats. Given the prevailing culture of toughness, negative consequences of such exposure may remain unacknowledged, undiagnosed and/or untreated. This may lead to gradual erosion of staff's wellness, professionalism, and job performance.

11. **Socio-cultural and political contexts.** Staff often feel devalued by the general public. They might not experience much respect as an honorable branch of criminal justice. They may

experience negative stereotyping in the media instead, due to the acts of a few. The negative impact of the work is rarely acknowledged, and their successes or life-saving acts are rarely publicly recognized. Corrections may also be viewed by legislators as a fiscal "black hole," and expected to "do more with less."

12. **Insufficient training.** Corrections work is highly complex. Basic training at the academy, followed by some additional hours of annual training, are not enough to sufficiently equip staff to excel at performing their seemingly ever evolving corrections duties. Insufficient training may result in staff making serious errors, possibly endangering lives, and facing investigations, discipline, perhaps the loss of their career, and even legal action.

13. **Violations and revocations.** Following client violations, probation/parole agents must implement interventions or recommend revocation. These decisions are sometimes made while in clients' homes, and while dealing with reactions of clients and their families–which can be distressing and dangerous. If revocation is requested but denied by the court, probation/parole agents feel invalidated and unsupported by the judicial system. In addition to safety concerns, they experience a loss of credibility

and authority with clients they continue to supervise. Additionally, they may become uncertain as to how to best handle future violations.

EFFECTS OF CORRECTIONS FATIGUE

Corrections Fatigue brings about negative changes in staff's personality, health, functioning, core beliefs, and ideology. When sufficiently high numbers of staff are thus affected, the entire workplace culture bears the marks of Corrections Fatigue. These changes interact and are self-reinforcing, setting up "vicious cycles" that worsen factors that contribute to Corrections Fatigue. As a corrections professional once quipped, "We don't only suffer from Corrections Fatigue; we also cause it in others."

PERSONALITY CHANGES

Corrections Fatigue is proposed to negatively affect the following areas of a person's self: identity, worldview, spirituality, emotions, and behaviors.

Identity: As a result of Corrections Fatigue, staff may experience themselves rigidly and one-dimensionally as law enforcers, heroes, rescuers, or victims. Thought patterns associated with Corrections Fatigue may include: *"I'm a warrior;" "I'm a savior;" "I'm a glorified waiter/babysitter;" "I'm a human doormat."*

Worldview: The lens through which corrections

staff view the world becomes distorted. They may end up perceiving others as dangerous, dishonest, untrustworthy, or just plain "bad people." They may disrespect and dislike whoever differs from them. To avoid getting exploited or hurt, they try to stay in control and ahead of any "games." Thought patterns associated with Corrections Fatigue may include: *"You can't trust anybody;" "Watch out or they'll play you;" "It's me (us) against them."*

Spirituality: Over time, corrections staff may have difficulty enjoying beauty, purity and innocence, and/or experiencing love, affection and compassion. And they may become plagued with a sense of meaninglessness and futility about their work and life. Thought patterns associated with Corrections Fatigue include: *"Life sucks;" "There's no such thing as true love;" "Kindness is weakness."*

Emotions: Emotions associated with Corrections Fatigue include those on the anger continuum (ranging from irritability to rage), hate, anxiety, fear, sadness, helplessness, guilt and shame. Other emotional states are indifference and "emotional numbing."

Behaviors: Behaviors typically associated with Corrections Fatigue are impatience; intolerance; high degrees of control; verbal and/or physical aggression; social withdrawal; and addictions to substances or processes, such as alcohol, tobacco, prescription or illegal drugs, gambling, or sexual compulsivity.

HEALTH

The relentless pounding of corrections occupational stressors on staff's body, soul, and spirit takes its toll.

Consequences on the staff's bodies include cardio-vascular diseases; gastro-intestinal disorders; Type 2 diabetes; sleep disturbances; and obesity.

Psychological consequences can include the development of symptoms of depression, post-traumatic stress, generalized anxiety, and/or panic disorder.

Health conditions can undermine staff's energy level, and their ability to concentrate, remember, reason, problem-solve, or make sound decisions—all of which are critical for good job performance.

CORE BELIEFS ABOUT SEVEN KEY PSYCHOLOGICAL AREAS

Negative changes that comprise Corrections Fatigue also involve staff's core beliefs in seven areas, which in turn affect staff's behavior. These areas are physical safety, psychological safety, trust, power, respect, connection, and meaning.

Due to occupational experiences, staff may feel physically unsafe both on and off the job; feel psychologically/socially unsafe around coworkers; become mistrusting; feel powerless or all-powerful; feel disrespected and be disrespectful towards others; feel and/or choose to remain emotionally disconnected; and perceive their work to be meaningless.

Consequently, the workplace ideology espouses beliefs such as, "It's us against them;" "Get them before they get you;" "Never trust anyone;" "Offenders are treated better than we are;" "Nobody cares;" "It's all a farce and a waste." When new hires, full of zest, walk into "fatigued" workplaces, they are shocked by the negativity there. If not mentored wisely, they risk becoming disillusioned about the profession, and may start to manifest similar signs themselves.

These seven key areas are interrelated. Affecting one eventually influences the rest. We'll revisit these seven areas in the next chapter.

HOW ONE OFFICER MAINTAINS A POSITIVE WORK ATTITUDE IN A NEGATIVE WORK ENVIRONMENT

Inmates are young and old, black, white, Latino. They are sometimes psychotic, sociopathic, or social misfits. They are incarcerated for crimes such as: homicide, sexual assault, or drug use or dealing. Some are very bad people; some have just made bad choices, but are basically good people.

We have authority over them and inmates must comply with the rules of the institution. However, there is a great amount of latitude in how a correctional officer may interact with an inmate.

To many of my coworkers, these inmates are all people who do not deserve anything, because their own actions led to their incarceration. They see them as less than human. They may be treated with indifference and might even be ignored when they ask for something. There is a definite "us vs. them" attitude.

I have found that a correctional officer can have a direct impact on their work environment. How we interact with others on a daily basis can make a great deal of difference in how stressful our lives will become. Everyone wants to be treated with dignity and respect, regardless of who they are or what their charges may be. Take the time to learn the names of those you are working with. Try to look at them as individuals, without passing judgment. Our job is to make sure that the inmates are safe and secure, that they do not harm themselves or anyone else, and that they are not harmed by others. There is a judicial system that has or will

judge them and determine their guilt or inno-
cence. We are not social workers; however, we
can make a difference in their lives by how we
conduct ourselves.

Take a minute and talk with them when they ask
questions. By taking the time to respond to their
basic needs or answer a simple question, you show
them respect. This does not mean you can't say no.
However, when a request is reasonable and falls
within our facility's rules and regulations, there is
no reason not to respond to them. If they see you
as willing to work with them, they are usually more
cooperative when you make demands or requests
of them. If you are not facing confrontations on a
daily basis, stress levels will decrease and you will
not find yourself taking your anger and frustration
home with you each night.

Ours is a dangerous job. We can't let our guard
down. But we can reduce stress levels by being less
negative and conducting ourselves in a profession-
al manner. Many correctional officers use up too
much energy trying to prove they are in charge,
and may come across as more confrontational
than they need to be. By using the communication
skills most of us have learned on the job,
we can create a more positive and less stressful
work environment.

~Jail Deputy

HOW NEGATIVE CHANGES HAPPEN OVER TIME

Corrections Fatigue does not happen overnight. Here are phases that staff may go through as they struggle to adapt to challenges of corrections work.

The "Honeymoon" Phase: New employees are on a "high." They are excited and motivated, ready to make a difference through their new profession. Their self-esteem is soaring. Administrators are congratulating them and urging them on, and their loved ones are proud of them.

The "Work Immersion" Phase: Rookies begin to climb a steep learning curve as they encounter the job's operational complexities and inter-personal dynamics with staff and offenders. Characteristics of this phase include:

1. Being consumed by the job, working hard to earn staff's respect and acceptance;
2. Volunteering for overtime and special assignments;
3. Longing to do something exceptional, even heroic;
4. Feeling exhilarated for belonging in the corrections family; and
5. Defining themselves by their profession.

At this point staff's families may start feeling like they have been left behind. Staff may share little about their work experiences. Describing corrections work to someone who's never done it is difficult. Staff may also not want to cause their family undue worry. Shift work and overtime add to the much reduced waking time spent with family. Special events are missed. Emotional gaps may begin to emerge in family relationships. And—let's face it—to staff, home life may now seem boring compared to the adrenaline highs at work.

The "Bubble Bursting" Phase: Sooner or later, an unpleasant occurrence happens that "bursts the employee's bubble." Bubble-bursting experiences may include:

1. Becoming embroiled in conflict with other staff;
2. Being physically assaulted by offenders;
3. Being disciplined for policy violations;
4. Witnessing a particularly violent incident; and
5. Not being selected for a team or a promotion.

As a result of bubble-bursting, staff might feel hurt, betrayed, anxious, discouraged, angry, humiliated, or persecuted. Other staff may be now viewed as "the enemy," and no longer be trusted. Passion for the profession wanes. For some, the bubble-bursting experience may be so shattering that they leave corrections. Others continue charging bravely ahead, keeping their misgivings to themselves. (It is perfectly appropriate for some staff to quit corrections work. Not everyone is "cut out" for this profession.)

The "Wall Building" Phase: If the bubble-bursting experience is not resolved successfully, or if such experiences keep happening, staff build self-protective "walls" to defend themselves from further hurt. However, unprocessed distress, disillusionment and resentment continue to accumulate behind these walls. Employees interact with as few staff as possible, trying to remain "under the radar." They may only vent to other embittered employees, but without identifying positive solutions. "Attitude" issues increase the probability of further bubble-bursting. The risk of errors or unprofessional behavior increases. Even constructive corrective feedback is poorly accepted at this point. Some staff may decide to quit. Others might be terminated for poor performance or misconduct.

The "Corrections Fatigue" Phase: In the absence of effective coping strategies, staff's negativity becomes entrenched. Employees might find themselves experiencing anxiety, anger, bitterness, vengefulness, hopelessness, mistrust, alienation, powerlessness and meaninglessness about the job—

and perhaps even about life itself. Some decide to quit corrections, and others may be terminated.

The "Crossroads" Phase: Staff are faced with choices. Will they elect to stay in the Corrections Fatigue zone (or quit their jobs), or will they commit to learn how to climb out of the Fatigue hole and find fulfillment again? The latter option takes courage and determination, and may involve seeking help from peers or professionals. To stop sinking deeper into the pit of Corrections Fatigue, and to take the fulfillment road, staff need to learn to:

1. Process/work through distressing work experiences;
2. Develop effective self-care skills;
3. Develop effective emotion-regulating skills;
4. Develop effective interpersonal skills;
5. Develop effective social support systems; and
6. Re-discover and even expand the positive meaning of their career.

As staff negotiate this phase, they can begin to move past Corrections Fatigue. In doing so, they help themselves, their workplace culture, and their families.

Of course, a corrections career involves more than the above phases. There are also stretches where employees are adapting to work demands effectively, are balancing work and home life well, and are enjoying periods of relative calm and job satisfaction.

Even the best-adjusted staff experience ups and downs, and may go through these phases numerous times throughout their career. Ideally, after each round, they become better at getting from bubble-bursting back to fulfillment. And changes in positions, duties, facilities, or personnel may help them start over with the Honeymoon phase.

Here are some suggestions for staff to recover faster following bubble-bursting experiences:

1. Accept that challenges happen even to the best in the profession—do not take them personally;
2. Try to understand the reasons why bubble-bursting happened, identify their part, if any, that may have contributed to the situation, and problem-solve effectively; and
3. View *every* experience as a personal growth opportunity.

Such practices result in the development of resilience—the capacity to recover and even make progress after disappointments, defeats, or dreadful experiences.

This booklet is intended to provide you with a positive Crossroads experience. May reading it prompt you to begin charting your own map down the corrections fulfillment road.

So how can you combat Corrections Fatigue and en-joy fulfillment at work, while maintaining a healthy personal life? Correcting thought patterns that become distorted by Corrections Fatigue, and practicing effective self-care are two ways to accomplish these goals. It is to these that we now turn our attention.

Reflection
What can you tell yourself next time you have a bubble-bursting experience?

---

[1]McCann, I. L., & Pearlman, L. A. (1990).
Psychological trauma and the adult survivor:
Theory, therapy, and transformation. New York: Bruner/Mazel.

[2]Saakvitne, K.W., & Pearlman, L.A. (1996).
Transforming the Pain. New York: Norton.

CHAPTER 3
TAKING YOUR LIFE BACK

Building and maintaining a healthy professional and personal life require correcting thoughts affected by Corrections Fatigue and implementing effective self-care strategies. In this chapter, you will find some suggestions for how to do this.

"REPAIRING" THOUGHT DISTORTIONS ABOUT SELF, THE WORLD AND LIFE

As mentioned earlier, Corrections Fatigue damages our beliefs about ourselves, other people, and our spirituality. Here are some ways to mend the damage:

Identity
- You are much more than your job. Your job is what you do, not who you are.
- You have many "parts" that make up who you are (e.g., spouse, parent, child, corrections professional, sports player, volunteer).
- Make sure you alternately and regularly engage all your various "parts."
- Remind yourself: *"Corrections is what I do eight hours a day—not who I am." "It's not my job to keep everyone under control 24/7."*

Worldview

- There are MANY upright, honest, and caring people in the world.
- There are many perspectives, and all may have valid points.
- Look for exceptions to your sweeping generalizations. You cannot accurately generalize from a few to "everyone."
- Some rules of operation in the corrections world do not apply to the "free" world.
- Remind yourself: *"There ARE good people out there;" "Some people DO get better;" "I will judge each person on their own merit."*

Spirituality

- Adopt positive values and principles to live by.
- Risk depending upon something bigger than yourself.
- Give, love, help, and be thankful.
- Adopt a positive spiritual framework, which also addresses the issue of evil.
- Remind yourself: *"I value optimism, integrity, honesty, kindness, and compassion;" "I am in awe of the beauty of nature;" "Goodness, love, and truth do win in the end."*

REPAIRING THE DAMAGE TO SEVEN KEY PSYCHOLOGICAL NEEDS AT WORK

As mentioned in the prior chapter, due to Corrections Fatigue, seven interrelated psychological needs become negatively affected. These are physical safety, psychological safety, trust, power, respect, connection, and meaning.

Here now is some more information about these areas, and suggestions for satisfying them effectively.

1. Physical safety. Corrections staff need to perceive that they are relatively safe from physical harm and that necessary precautions have been taken to attain that. Yet, corrections work is inherently unsafe. The potential for physical danger is ever-present. The perception of physical safety can also be compromised by exposure to life-threatening incidents or threats; understaffing; faulty or non-existent equipment or supplies; and staff weariness, inattentiveness, over-confidence, or indifference.

The sense of physical safety is increased when teamwork is good; staff perceive coworkers to be engaged, attentive, and well-rested; necessary equipment and supplies are available and functional; and staff-to-offender ratios are good.

2. Psychological safety. This is about how psychologically/socially safe or comfortable corrections employees feel around OTHER STAFF (NOT offenders). Lack of psychological safety creates social anxiety, avoidance behaviors, and/or conflict.

Psychological safety gets destroyed in workplaces where staff spread negative rumors, betray confidences unrelated to security issues, ridicule others, act spitefully, exploit, harass, or retaliate against coworkers.

In psychologically-safe environments, staff receive appropriate support when they seek it. When in distress, they are encouraged and comforted by coworkers. Colleagues honor confidences unrelated to security. And supervisors offer corrective feedback constructively, with helpful tips for performance improvement.

3. Trust. Trust is the glue that bonds people together. People who feel psychologically safe can begin to trust.

Corrections staff learn that trusting the wrong person could cost them their reputation, their careers, their freedom, and even their life. So they may come to believe that no one should be trusted. This leads to interpersonal isolation and a state of excessive vigilance and anxiety. Additionally, staff that have experienced fear, "froze," lost their self-control, or crossed policy lines may no longer trust themselves.

Trust is earned by staff who are consistent, knowledgeable and reliable; who keep promises; who act honorably and honestly; who are helpful; who respond to emergencies; and who show that they have staff's best interests at heart. Trustworthy individuals confront exploitation, abuse, or harassment of others, and make genuine attempts to resolve friction with coworkers.

4. Power. Personal power is about the ability to impact one's environment through being able to control oneself, make decisions, initiate behaviors, problem-solve, and give input in situations.

Corrections staff are expected to be in complete control of offenders. Yet they may have little input on issues that impact them directly, being expected to follow orders unquestioningly. And they cannot even control whether they go home at the end of their workday. Alternatively, some staff may abuse their power when interacting with offenders or other employees.

The legitimate need for power is met appropriately in work environments where leaders are comfortable with delegating responsibilities, and with receiving feedback from subordinates. It is also satisfied where abuses of power are not tolerated. Empowerment is also experienced through self-control—the ability to regulate one's emotions and actions when provoked or under pressure.

5. Respect. The need for respect involves the desire to be treated with decency, civility and fairness, regardless of rank, discipline, or status. Showing respect stems from valuing others as human beings.

Staff may be disrespected by offenders or other staff. Staff may not even respect themselves. In addition, the general public is mostly unaware of what corrections work involves, and may have little respect for corrections professionals.

Respect emanates from unconditional positive regard toward others, and aims to preserve their dignity. Respect is shown through words, facial expression, and tone of voice; through listening to others' opinions; by the way greetings are exchanged; and by the way others' presence is acknowledged.

6. Connection. This refers to the need for social support, belonging, camaraderie, and emotional intimacy. We are social creatures. Healthy attachments are vital to our well-being. We need relationships where others know at least some parts of the true "us" and accept us anyway, even while they offer suggestions to help us improve.

Oftentimes, corrections staff operate alone. In some assignments the opportunity to interact with coworkers is minimal. Staff remain emotionally isolated for long periods, resulting in loneliness and perhaps even anxiety. Consequently, to meet their yearning for social connection, they might gravitate towards offenders, or get entangled in inappropriate relationships with coworkers. On the other hand, if the prevailing workplace culture is one of low psychological safety and mistrust, staff might intentionally avoid connecting with coworkers, opting to operate behind psychological walls and fences.

Given the hours spent at work, it is critical that staff's need for connection be met appropriately and ethically on the job. Healthy teamwork, working through disagreements, being listened to, social events, appropriate caring, and demonstrations of support are ways to increase connection with coworkers within professional boundaries.

7. Meaning. Corrections staff need to know that what they do has significance—that they make a positive difference.

When staff's sense of professional meaning is suffering, they lose pride in their career, do not value coworkers, and come to believe that they are wasting their lives. Employees do not see a finished product at the end of each work day; they do not often hear about lasting positive outcomes to offenders' correctional experiences; and they may remain unaware of incidents prevented because of their vigilance. Without such directly observable evidence, and given the "revolving door" of recidivism, it may be hard for staff to believe that their pro-social efforts have lasting positive effects on offenders.

Corrections staff need to be shown regularly and through examples how their efforts do in fact have lasting, positive effects on others (staff or offenders). For that to be possible, success may have to be redefined as small steps in the right direction. Staff also need to remember that even one success story matters, and that they may never learn about offenders' progress.

Additionally, staff can satisfy their need for meaning by pursuing their own professional development, and by assisting other staff, such as through formal or informal mentoring, to develop professionally.

When staff work toward satisfying these seven areas in the workplace, they build each other up, bolster teamwork, role model pro-social behaviors to offenders, and create a safer environment for all.

THE ABCS OF SELF-CARE
To "detox" from Corrections Fatigue and enjoy their life when away from work, staff need healthy self-care strategies.

1. Awareness

You, as a corrections professional, are excellent at situational awareness, that is, awareness of your external environment. What is addressed here is "internal" awareness, being aware of yourself through observing your thoughts, emotions and body sensations, and doing so objectively and non-judgmentally. Acknowledging your "inner life" moment by moment, and in an accepting manner, gives you valuable information about what is going on with you and what you need. Practicing such acknowledgment can also help you calm down.

2. Balance

- Practice healthy transition strategies, from work to home and from home to work
- Balance thinking about work and detaching from the work mode
- Balance work and rest/relaxation/play
- Balance time for yourself and time for your loved ones
- Balance spending time indoors and time outdoors
- Balance venting about frustrations and celebrating what is going well
- Balance judgment and mercy, strictness and compassion
- Balance being in charge at home and letting others be in charge

3. Connection

- Have a healthy support system that may include family, friends, spiritual communities, support groups, pets, hobbies, and sports teams
- Confide in one or more trusted people
- LISTEN to others
- Seek to help and support others
- Engage in activities that nurture your spirit
- Invest time daily in your loved ones
- Make respect, empathy, thanksgiving, and caring the basis of your relationships

4. Discipline

- Make time for self-nurturing activities
- Intentionally practice optimistic thinking
- Intentionally practice gratitude and thankfulness
- Intentionally practice compassion
- Intentionally practice respectful communication
- Be on the lookout for negative thinking and correct it promptly
- Maintain healthy personal boundaries

Here are some basic behaviors that must also be on your list in order to stay well.

- Get enough sleep
- Eat regular and healthy meals
- Get regular physical exercise
- Smile
- Practice paced breathing

- Cut back on TV, computer games, and video games
- Have annual medical check-ups

We shall next address the nature of stress, and how to counter its effects.

Reflection

What is one simple health-promoting behavior that you are willing and able to start practicing TODAY to take better care of yourself?

CHAPTER 4
WE HAVE MET THE ENEMY

It is estimated that 60-80% of visits to primary care physicians include a stress-related component.[1] That is, 60-80% of common illnesses may be due to what we loosely call "stress."

It seems that even though we understand more than ever before the mechanisms through which "stress" can affect us, we are not doing as good of a job managing it and countering its long-term poisonous effects.

Some of us even scoff at the idea that "stress" can affect us negatively. We may instead proclaim that "stress" helps us focus, energizes us, and keeps us vigilant and on our toes. And I've heard corrections staff chuckle and say, "I don't HAVE stress! I GIVE stress!"

And yet, the verdict is in about the outcomes of exposure to chronic and/or extreme "stress." The stress response impacts a large number of body functions. As a result, vital organs such as the brain, the digestive system, the cardiovascular system, the immune system, the liver, the pancreas and the skin are affected.

Why is stress so detrimental to health?

In essence, the stress response involves mobilizing the body's resources to fend off a threat, anything that threatens the organism's survival or that threatens to throw it off balance in its performing its routine operations required for living.

We're familiar with the term "fight or flight" which is triggered by part of our autonomic nervous system. We're less familiar with another term—"rest and digest," which is run by another part of our autonomic nervous system. This refers to functions that the body runs quietly in the background, humming away, to keep us alive, such as breathing, the beating of our heart and blood circulation, digestion, and temperature control.

"Fight or flight" reactions derail "rest and digest" functions, in their attempt to cope with danger. That of course can be a life saver when there is a real physical threat to our survival.

Some examples of the stress response outcomes are interrupted digestion, increased heart rate and blood pressure, increased blood circulation to large muscles (arms and legs), released cholesterol in the blood stream, slight thickening of the blood, re-leased glucose (sugar) from the liver into the blood stream, increased inflammation, or suppression of immune system functions.

These aspects of the stress response are designed to deal with external dangers that can result in physical injuries, or internal threats, like viral or bacterial infections.

However, social (psychological or emotional) threats elicit the very same stress response that physical threats do. It is as if our brains have only a hammer as a tool to deal with danger, and so, to our brains, every threat—whether physical or so-cial—is a nail.

That is, confrontations with coworkers or super-visors will produce the same set of body changes as would a confrontation with a wooly mammoth. Strong emotions, such as anger, anxiety or grief, elicit the stress response in the body just like an en-counter with a dinosaur would. And, furthermore, it does not matter to the brain if an event has really happened or not. An imagined or anticipated dread-ed occurrence can result in the same flood of stress chemicals as an actual event. Fear of being found guilty during an investigation, fear of retaliation due to filing a grievance, or resentment felt when a perceived injustice is remembered—all lead to the same "fight or flight" stress response in the body. We can be vacationing in a most relaxing part of the world, and yet ruin our mood just by remembering or thinking about events that trigger hate, resentment, worry, or sadness in us.

So what do you think happens to body tissues and organs if the stress response gets triggered over and over, perhaps several times a day, for periods of months or years? The body can handle an encounter with a sable-toothed tiger or an offender with a shank perhaps once every couple of years or so. As long as one survives the attack, the body will likely bounce back. But being subjected to the stress response several times daily, over and over, is another story.

What would happen to an engine if it was made to run for days at a time at the highest end of RPMs that is was designed for, or when the engine was made to run outside the parameters for which it was designed? Most of us would say that the engine would end up with metal fatigue, with parts getting ground down or breaking off due to the friction, with the engine overheating, running out of oil, and eventually burning up.

This is, figuratively, what can happen to the body when the stress response takes place over and over. That is how diseases can start. The body may bounce back from stress-related chemicals that are secreted in it occasionally. When exposure to these chemicals is repeated often and becomes the norm, that's when the damage is likely to start happening, accumulating over time as the exposure continues unabated.

And what are corrections staff facing as "part of the job?" At the minimum, staff are overly vigilant, continually on high alert, which, by definition, means that the "fight or flight" mode has become chronic. Add to the mix confrontations with staff or offenders, critical incidents, near misses, investigations, work-home life imbalances, financial concerns, and frequent mandatory overtime, and it becomes rather obvious why perpetually stressed corrections employees may be prone to health conditions.

And that is why taking measures to embrace a lifestyle that decreases the stress response, while increasing time spent in the "rest and digest" mode can be a life saver.

Here are some basic approaches to achieve that. They may sound overly simplistic, but they work if you work them, especially if you practice them regularly.

- Breathe into your abdomen slowly and gently, and exhale deeply, focusing on your breath. Do this for at least 5 minutes daily, and also whenever you feel stressed.

- Eat slowly and chew your food well, paying attention to its taste and texture.
- Slow down and spend time in nature, observing all that is beautiful around you.
- Spend relaxing time with family and friends.
- Generate positive emotions, such as love, joy, and peace. Laugh. Express affection and compassion. Think of what you are grateful for, and express your gratitude. Forgive. Spend time imagining positive and lovely events and outcomes.
- Sing joyful songs, and listen to cheerful or calming music.
- Practice yoga or tai chi.
- Give yourself plenty of time when you go somewhere, to avoid hurrying.
- Take naps.

Reflection

What is a strategy you choose to practice daily to increase your "rest and digest" response?

[1] https://www.ncbi.nlm.nih.gov/pmc/articles/PMC4286362/

CHAPTER 5
PROFESSIONAL BOUNDARIES

Maintaining sound professional boundaries is mission-critical in corrections. Professional boundary violations harm not only the individuals involved, but also entire systems. Boundary violations give the public image of the corrections profession yet another black eye. They compromise the security of operations, as policies are broken and self-interest overtakes public interest. And they demoralize coworkers.

Disillusionment and disgust follow after staff learn that staff they trusted or looked up to violated professional boundaries. Examples are when employees discover that staff they considered to be role models and even mentors violated policies, ranging from employee sexual harassment to inappropriate relationships with employees to inappropriate interactions with offenders. Associated actions can be retaliating against subordinates who reject their overtures, transmitting messages between offenders and others, introducing contraband, or aiding in an escape. Such behaviors are experienced by coworkers like "bubble-bursting" personal betrayals, and many of them have difficulty trusting or respecting fellow staff again.

What may be baffling to staff is that the perpetrators may have been "shining stars" or staff who performed reliably and honorably for years. Then, seemingly suddenly, they make unethical and perhaps illegal choices.

What is at the root of such destructive choice-making?

The root of unethical behavior is usually traced to the pursuit of self-gratification outside of what is allowed professionally. (Some people would say that such behavior is motivated by greed or lust.) This happens when basic urges, which drive us to need satisfaction, win over professional ethics.

Ethical conduct requires abiding by what has been determined to constitute legal, moral, and socially acceptable behavior. Pro-social behavior involves respecting the parameters within which we are to operate in order to not exploit or otherwise harm others. Many of these parameters are immutable, written in stone. Others fall in the grey zone, to be evaluated on a case-by-case basis. For example, in today's corrections, personal involvement with offenders is never acceptable, and sexual involvement is grounds for prosecution through the

Prison Rape Elimination Act (PREA). On the other hand, in some jurisdictions flings with subordinates may be grounds for dismissal or a strongly urged resignation, whereas in other workplace cultures such behavior may be acceptable.

So how do professional boundary violations happen?

To convince ourselves to cross clearly stated professional boundaries, we must first convince ourselves through rationalizations why the behavior is permissible to us. Remember, our basic brain wiring drives us to satisfy our needs and wants. So if we are in a "needy" frame of mind, we may generate excuses for contemplated policy infractions. If temptations are seductive enough, we might tell ourselves that the existing rules are too rigid, that our case is an exception to the rule, that if it were wrong it would not feel so right, that we are being unfairly deprived of a good thing, that nobody will know, that nobody will get hurt, that our family needs the money, that we are poorly paid for the job, that this is a once in a lifetime opportunity, etc., etc.

While sliding down the slippery slope toward boundary violations, we are mesmerized by the prospect of having "it." We are certain that "it" will ensure our happiness and satisfaction. So we downplay or ignore potential costs of our choices.

The hook, the root of such disastrous choices, is talking ourselves into believing the lie that there is something outside the proscribed boundaries which is wildly desirable and much better than what we have or what is allowed. We get hooked when we start feeling unjustly deprived—that rewards and other good things are being unfairly withheld from us by "life," administrators, society, or circumstances. When such thoughts are coupled with rationalizations that no one will get hurt by our misconduct and that nobody will know, then it is only a matter of time before the next step is taken—that of professional boundary violations to meet personal wants or needs.

So the concealed hook is the falsehood that the "forbidden fruit" is much superior to what we already have, that we are being "done wrong" by having it withheld from us, and that breaking some rules to get our hands on it is justifiable—and harmless.

The reality though is that the workplace is absolutely not the proper venue to meet personal needs through offenders or even staff in many cases. Yes, in some cases staff rejected by coworkers, with their needs for connection and respect left unmet, end up gravitating towards offenders. However, two wrongs don't make a right. Getting personally involved with offenders only leads to more woe.

"Insurance" against self-deception is found in unquestioning adherence to policies and ethical guidelines, and acceptance that they are there for good reason—even if that reason is obscure to us at this time. The key is acceptance of limits and respect for rules without trying to find loopholes to "beat the system."

"Insurance" against boundary violations is also based on character maturity—on sound values, the capacity to control personal urges and forego unethical self-gratification, and the willingness to honestly foresee consequences to one's choices. To remain ethical, staff must be ready to reject ego strokes, or unethical or illegal monetary or other rewards. Wise staff know that, indeed, all that glitters is not gold.

Boundaries exist to protect staff's effectiveness in carrying out professional duties; to safeguard staff's career, reputation, and self-respect; to safeguard the quality of social interactions in corrections settings; and to protect staff's health, and even their very lives.

In summary, pro-social thinking, self-honesty, and self-discipline are needed to remain ethical in corrections. The only way to avoid getting hooked is to not play with the bait.

Reflection

Write down your main emotional needs,
and what you are doing to satisfy
them appropriately.

CHAPTER 6
A FAMILY AFFAIR

When Desert Waters started serving corrections staff and their families in 2003, the wife of a corrections officer told me, "When my husband got a job at the Department of Corrections as an officer, I had no idea that we'd be signing up too, as a family." And a corrections professional's husband told me, tongue-in-cheek, "Since my wife started working in Corrections, our lives have changed drastically— forever. Now we refer to 'life B.C.' (before corrections) and 'life A.C.' (after corrections). Some 'A.C.' things I like, some not so much, and some not at all."

Over the years, I've heard similar statements expressed by partners of corrections staff who find themselves trying to navigate the uncharted waters of their loved one's new profession.

More often than not, partners and other family members enter the world of corrections unprepared for the emotional toll this occupation can take on you, and by extension on them, and the changes they will be faced with as a result of your job demands.

They are happy that you get a steady paycheck with benefits. They are thrilled to hear that your paycheck is augmented through the shift work pay differential, working on holidays, and overtime.

But your loved ones do not yet know how your family's rhythms, traditions, and practices will be affected by the nature and demands of corrections work, and what they can do about that. They are not aware of lifestyle changes that shift work, overtime and changing work schedules bring, and they are not mentally and practically prepared for the sacrifices that these changes require.

Your partner does not know that, with your entry in the corrections workforce, they too will be entering a world where things happen that are so far out of the ordinary, that if they were told to people on the street, many would just not believe them.

Partners also do not know that the corrections job you just started will come home with you. They are not aware of how, in addition to you acquiring desirable new skills due to working in corrections, you might also be shaped negatively by the job, becoming someone quite unlike who you used to be prior to starting your corrections career.

Most partners do not know or understand corrections agencies' policies and procedures, administrative regulations, work circumstances and details, the jargon used, or what it is like to work all night and try to sleep during the day. They do not understand the power dynamics of the paramilitary corrections culture. Unless they themselves or their parents have worked in corrections, law enforcement or in the military, they have no frame of reference for your work experiences.

Your partner does not know that their ability to intimately "connect" with you may decrease as the years go by, with the possible outcome that eventually you two might become strangers at the emotional level. Conversations stay shallow, superficial, with you usually answering the question, "How was your day?" with "Fine," regardless of what has actually happened that day at work. After a while, your partner may feel like it is useless for them to ask you about your workday. Due to your emotional distancing—living behind psychological walls even when at home—they can conclude that they no longer know who you are becoming, or that you no longer want them to be a part of your life.

Your partner is not prepared to deal with your being chronically tired or even exhausted, not having the energy or motivation to do much when off work. They do not understand why you no longer want to engage with the children or help out. And that may lead to conflict, and to your adding a few more bricks to your wall.

Your partner is not prepared to deal with you becoming more impatient, irritable, or prone to angry outbursts for no apparent reason; and so they may snap back at you. This can end up in verbal clashes that you are likely to win, just because you are well practiced at doing so at work. Only the victory at home comes with a steep price tag of emotional distancing and something dying inside after each fight. And the fact that your fuse keeps getting shorter ends up scaring your loved ones. So, they may avoid spending time with you or discussing sensitive or controversial family matters. Again, with time, more walls get erected between you and them. Your partner does not expect to see you steadily gaining weight, with your blood pressure and blood sugar readings no longer falling in the normal range.

Your partner does not expect you to keep increasing your level of alcohol consumption, or to begin to engage in other escapist behaviors, such as excessive playing of video games, gambling, or online sexual activities. Similarly, your partner is not prepared to deal with your starting to show signs of serious anxiety, depression, or post-traumatic stress.

Your newly developed gallows humor may be appalling to them, rendering you not very likeable to them, and perhaps even repulsive.

Similarly, the sky-rocketing increase in your use of

profanity, often regardless of who is present, can shock them.

Your partner has no idea why you are becoming harder, more calloused, or judgmental of others. Your seeming indifference towards instances of injury or death of offenders or others, your apparent lack of compassion, troubles them. Your cutting, uncaring or merciless comments about people stun them. ("Is this the man I married?" "Is this who my wife is becoming?")

The way you at times talk to strangers in public—curtly, perhaps even aggressively, and obviously assuming the worst about them—may cause your partner public embarrassment. Once again they think that you are being unnecessarily critical and judgmental, biased against certain groups of people, and that you are no longer kind, considerate or objective. This translates into their finding you to not be likeable—which can lead to friction between you, and more emotional distancing.

Your partner finds it insulting and hurtful that at times you talk down to them as if they are offenders—ordering them around, giving them a threatening look during an argument, and trying to control their every move.

Your partner might also get fed up with your objections as to why the family cannot go to certain places or associate with certain people, thinking that you are simply overreacting. They find your increasing caution and concerns about danger, and your pervasive mistrust of people (which, in their estimation, borders on paranoia) annoying at best, interfering with normal social functioning, and creating verbal clashes at home.

Your partner does not understand why you are increasingly stricter with your children, overly worried about their safety, laying down rigid rules, and wanting to run background checks on their friends and their parents. Your partner cringes when you exclaim, "None of MY kids will become inmates!"

Your partner might get tired of going to family gatherings, school events, or other social activities alone, feeling more like a single parent than a partner in a marriage, raising the children and running the household on their own—no longer enjoying the teamwork they used to have with you.

Even sharing the bed with you (when they get to do that) can pose its own problems, as you may have punched or kicked your partner in the middle of the night during a nightmare, while dreaming that you are fighting off offenders.

These issues, left unaddressed, take their toll on corrections marriages and on parent-child relationships.

So, what can you do? Let's start small, exactly where you're at. Pick a good time to share this chapter with your loved one. And the chapter after it. Talk about these topics in small chunks. Ask your partner to tell you about their experiences with you. Find out to what degree they relate to what's stated in these chapters. Also find out what they are happy about, what in their opinion is going well in your relationship. When do they feel most connected with you emotionally? What are they satisfied about in your marriage?

If life at home has been tense for a while, your partner may not be ready to open up to you right away, as they may be apprehensive about your getting upset or angry at them. Give them time and space, and keep repeating your desire to have more meaningful and more intimate conversations. You'll need to earn your partner's trust, that you indeed want to help make home life better.

Again, when the time is right, share with them the rest of this booklet. And after that, find other materials to read together and discuss with your partner, such as articles posted on Desert Waters' site (http://desertwaters.com, under ezine—the Correctional Oasis).

If your conversations with your partner show you that your relationship has suffered some deep wounds, please consider looking into couples' counseling.

The bottom line is reconnecting with your partner—opening your heart to them again and letting them in. Keep taking small steps in that direction. These steps will add up, and get you where you need to be going.

Reflection
What can you do, starting today, to help improve your communication with your partner?

CHAPTER 7
TO TALK OR NOT TO TALK

As stated in the prior chapter, family members are usually unaware of what corrections work entails and how it may affect their loved one. The following is a typical communication I get from significant others of corrections staff:

"My husband, a corrections officer, used to be fun and full of energy. Now, after five years in corrections, he's grouchy and tired all the time. And he puts me down a lot. We don't go out much anymore, and when we do, he has to sit with his back against the wall and watch everybody. He just can't relax. Please help me understand what happened to him!"

To be able to be supportive of their loved ones, partners need a road map, ways to understand how such changes come about.

When Work Starts to Affect Your Family Life
Does the following scenario sound familiar?

You've dragged yourself through another shift. As you crawl into your vehicle, you say to yourself,

"I made it another day!" As you peel away from the gate, hateful words and confrontations replay in your mind. You drive down the road, screaming inside your head at offenders and other staff, wishing you could take a swing at someone or kick something. You know you will be home in thirty minutes. Just the thought of having to deal with one more person makes you tense up even more. You're not looking forward to any "Hi, honey. How was your day?" chatter. How will you handle getting home this time?

Once again, you review your options. When you make it out of the prison gate, you want to leave work behind. You wish you could step in the shower and wash yourself clean from the crud of the workday. You want to get on with YOUR life. Not too long from now you will have to climb into that uniform again and head back to the gate. You don't want to contaminate your "free" time with thoughts about the ugliness of work. You also don't want to upset your partner with your frustrations or fears. You don't even want to put your feelings into words. A couple of beers should drown them and keep them out of sight.

Trying to forget what you've just been through at work gives you short-term relief, temporary reprieve from the bombardment of work pressures. Not talking about work allows you to engage in normal, free-world activities. Perhaps you can do something with the kids or watch television. Your family can continue their regular routine without worrying about you and your work life.

"What good would it do to talk, anyway?" you tell yourself. You want to protect your loved ones, to spare them knowing how rough things can get at work. Burdening your partner with your work-day's struggles would only cause them needless worry. Your partner cannot do anything to fix the situation, anyway.

Besides, you don't want your partner Monday-morning quarterbacking you. You don't want to hear comments like: "You shouldn't have said that," "You're going to get yourself fired, and then what?" "I want to talk to that guy myself," or "This is what you need to do next time!" You have enough criticism at work. You don't need to bring more upon yourself at home. You've already got one boss. So, if you don't talk, you won't get lectured or yelled at again at home—at least not for your work performance.

And even if your partner is supportive, you tell yourself that they cannot really understand the corrections culture and its politics (unless they've worked in corrections too). That gives you one more reason to not open up.

You also don't talk because sometimes you can't. There are cases under investigation that you cannot discuss.

And yet you cannot deny the fact that as a couple you are drifting apart. You can't even remember the last time you had a heart-to-heart talk. There are many empty emotional spaces between the two of you. This worries you when you think about it. Your job is changing you, and you are becoming a stranger to your partner.

Besides, when you get honest with yourself, you have to admit that you do bring your troubles home. Yes, you don't talk about what happens at work. Instead, you blow up over usually insignificant "stuff." You complain, criticize, pick fights, and order people around. Or you hang out at the bar with your buddies after work, and get home late—and your partner does not appreciate that.

There may be no simple solution to your dilemma—to talk or no to talk, and to what extent? But the undeniable reality is that you do need to share your heart with your partner—to let them "in"—if you are to stay emotionally connected. You need to learn how to share and discuss the impact of stressful work experiences, and good things that happen, too. And you need to do it in ways that do not violate confidentiality, and do not overwhelm your partner with worry about your welfare. Your relationship will likely benefit when your spouse has a better grasp of your professional life. Listen respectfully and compassionately to your partner's concerns. Hear them out, and offer reassurance, especially after a disturbance at your workplace makes the news. Lack of emotional intimacy at home puts you at risk of not only becoming strangers, but also becoming inappropriately involved with coworkers.

Here are some suggestions for increasing your emotional intimacy with your partner:

1. Educate your partner, slowly and patiently. Describe your work duties to them. Give them this booklet to read. Download past issues of Desert Waters' (http://desertwaters.com) ezine, the Correctional Oasis, for them to read. Purchase some of the other Desert Waters' booklets or them to read.

2. Talk about work experiences, focusing on your feelings, rather than incident details. Have meaningful conversations about how you are doing. For example, inform them of an offender/client death, how you feel about it (angry/sad/numb), and what you need from your partner now (alone time and/or a hug). Or share what went well, and how you feel about that. Celebrate successes together!

3. Ask your partner how they are impacted by your

sharing. Listen attentively to their answer. Comfort them if they express concern about your welfare. Answer questions, again focusing on your emotions and coping strategies.

4. If you come from a faith perspective, pray together, and pray for your partner daily.

5. After you talk about work, switch your focus to the present at home. Eat, laugh, play, relax, or do chores together.

For partners: If your loved one works in corrections, listen to them without trying to fix the situation. Be supportive by validating their emotions. Avoid overly simplistic reassurances, such as, "It'll all work out." Let your partner know it is okay to feel strongly about certain situations. Express your thanks and appreciation to your partner for sharing with you, and for taking care of you and your family by working in corrections. Pray for them.

Below are a few questions partners can ask of corrections professionals to increase emotional intimacy:

- How does your workday usually unfold?
- What are routine procedures, tasks, exchanges you have with other staff and offenders?
- What are some of the challenges you face at work?

- What are you expected to do in an emergency?
- What are some of your areas of concern about your work?
- What do you like about your job?
- What do you feel you're especially good at regarding your job role?
- What are some of the strengths of your teammates?
- What is your direct supervisor like?
- How can I help you leave work behind when you get home?
- How would you like me to support you around work-related issues?
- How can we talk about your work experiences enough so I stay close to you, but not too much, so you don't feel like you cannot get away from work when you get home?
- How would you like me to approach you when you seem to me to be overly consumed by work?

Reflection
What can you do to bridge emotional gaps in your relationships with your loved ones?

CHAPTER 8
PSYCHOLOGICAL TRAUMA

An inescapable occupational hazard of corrections work is exposure to various types of potentially traumatizing material. This is a serious matter, as research has established that traumatic exposure can have lasting negative effects on health and functioning.

Observations in wartime have shown than even the "toughest of the tough" can be affected by exposure to life-threatening events. Up to fairly recently, the corrections culture of toughness has tended to leave the issue of occupational trauma in the corrections "war zone" unaddressed. Being "tough" is essentially a requirement for the job—especially for security/ custody staff. Employees who experience or witness life-threatening incidents are expected to "get back on the horse" immediately, and continue functioning unscathed. This widely embraced expectation causes exposed staff to deny emotional struggles following traumatic events, to not appear "weak." Instead of seeking help, they may feel ashamed because they are still troubled by incidents. Women custody staff may struggle with this issue even more than the men, due to additional pressure to "prove their mettle" to male colleagues.

What types of potentially traumatic incidents might corrections staff be exposed to at work? Such events typically include: being physically assaulted; witnessing the injury or murder of coworkers or offenders, offender suicides or suicide attempts, or sexual assaults; responding to large group disturbances; or being part of an execution team. These are examples of *direct,* "first hand," exposure to potentially traumatic events. They involve either *experiencing/enduring oneself* or *witnessing* life-threatening events in real time.

Corrections staff's traumatic exposure is also *indirect* or "second hand." This occurs when staff hear or read about work-related life-threatening incidents, or view them electronically later on. Indirect traumatic exposure also occurs when staff learn about crimes offenders committed prior to their incarceration, or about traumatic events experienced by offenders prior to or during their incarceration. Threats of violence to oneself or family members is another type of indirect traumatic exposure.

The American Psychiatric Association's *Diagnostic and Statistical Manual for Mental Disorders, Fifth Edition* (DSM-5; 2013)[1] states that **both direct and indirect traumatic exposure can contribute to the development of Post-traumatic Stress Disorder (PTSD).** This is a neurobiological disorder, which, in addition to psychological symptoms, involves structural and functional brain changes.

In the case of first responders, repeated or extreme indirect forms of work-related traumatic exposure were said to possibly result in PTSD (DSM-5, p. 271).

Given the DSM-5's expanded definition of types of events that can result in PTSD (both direct and indirect), and given research findings[2] on the widespread traumatic exposure of corrections workers, it becomes obvious that corrections is a high-trauma occupation, like policing, firefighting, and military combat. Negative effects of multiple traumatic exposures accumulate, contributing to the build-up of Corrections Fatigue. Moreover, alarmingly often, corrections workers may be experiencing both PTSD and depression symptoms[3], which can be debilitating. This is particularly pronounced for security/custody staff whose job roles involve the most frequent and most direct exposure to traumatic events.

Increasingly more corrections agencies acknowledge the effects of traumatic exposure, and utilize peer support teams following potentially traumatic incidents. Such practices offer social support and validation to exposed staff, and can counter the reluctance to seek help.

DIAGNOSING PTSD
According to the DSM-5, PTSD presents four symptom clusters: intrusive remembering, avoidance, negative thoughts and mood, and increased arousal and reactivity.

Intrusive remembering. This category of symptoms refers to repeated and unwelcome remembering of trauma details. Involuntary remembering is spontaneous or cued by reminders in the person's external environment (for example, smells, sounds, people, situations), or in the person's internal environment (for example, thoughts). Memories are accompanied by intense emotional distress and physiological arousal, such as increased heart rate, shaking, or sweating. Flashbacks are a particularly disturbing type of intrusive remembering, when the person relives the event, as if it is happening again. Intrusive memories can be experienced both while awake and while asleep (nightmares).

Avoidance. This refers to the persistent, active, and intentional avoidance of both external and internal trauma reminders. Avoidance is an attempt to insulate oneself from "triggers" in the outer world and in one's own mind. Substance abuse may be one method of attempting to avoid/block/numb traumatic memories.

Negative thoughts and mood. These involve negative changes in one's thinking that become entrenched; negative conclusions about oneself and others; and the persistent experiencing of distressing emotions. Examples include persistent negative judgments of self or others; hopelessness; exaggerated or unfounded self-blame or blame of others regarding perceived causes or consequences of traumatic events; pervasive anger, fear, guilt, or shame; loss of interest in important activities; feelings of emotional detachment from others; and difficulty experiencing positive emotions, such as affection.

Increased arousal and reactivity. This refers to easily switching to a "fight or flight" mode, or to being chronically agitated, causing a person to be "on edge," and at times go "over the edge." Examples include irritability; anger outbursts; verbal or physical aggression; being on guard; an unusually strong startle reflex; difficulty concentrating; sleep disturbances; and reckless or self-destructive behaviors.

If a certain number of these symptoms exist, a trauma-exposed individual can be diagnosed with PTSD. For such a diagnosis, symptoms must result in significant functioning impairments socially, occupationally, or otherwise, and must last for more than one month.

If you work in corrections, you have most likely experienced at least one traumatic episode directly, and/or also encountered traumatic material indirectly, possibly repeatedly. You may still be bothered by these exposures, and might be experiencing some of the symptoms listed here. Remember, even the "toughest of the tough" show signs of wear-and-tear as the number and types of traumatic material to which they are exposed at work continue to accumulate.

If that is true for you, here are some suggestions:

1. Acknowledge that you are still bothered by extremely stressful situations to which you were exposed;

2. Talk to significant others, peers, or spiritual advisors about this;

3. Seek help from knowledgeable medical and/or behavioral health professionals;

4. Engage in activities that are health-promoting, body-calming, emotion-calming, and nurturing socially and spiritually, such as physical exercise, outdoors activities, psychotherapy, journaling, or attending support groups or faith-based gatherings; and

5. Abstain from substance abuse or other addictive behaviors.

Yes, you can work through traumatic experiences, and you can even grow in self-awareness, compassion, and appreciation of life and of relationships as a result of doing so.

Reflection

What are three ways to manage your emotions constructively following exposure to a work-related traumatic incident?

---

[1]American Psychiatric Association. (2013). *Diagnostic and statistical manual of mental disorders (DSM-5) (Fifth Ed.).* Washington D.C.: American Psychiatric Association.

[2]Spinaris, C.G., Denhof, M.D., & Kellaway, J.A. (2012). Posttraumatic Stress Disorder in United States Corrections Professionals: Prevalence and Impact on Health and Functioning. http://desertwaters.com/wp-content/uploads/2013/09/PTSD_Prev_in_Corrections_09-03-131.pdf

[3]Denhof, M.D., & Spinaris, C.G. (2013). Depression, PTSD, and Comorbidity in United States Corrections Professionals: Impact on Health and Functioning. http://desertwaters.com/wp-content/uploads/2013/09/Comorbidity_Study_09-03-131.pdf

CHAPTER 9
DEPRESSION

The disease of depression is biological and psychological in nature. It results from distressing life events, such as loss; prolonged stressful conditions; and/or genetics. Depression involves changes in brain chemistry and behavior.

Additionally, studies have shown that the following work conditions can increase the risk of developing depressive symptoms: high psychological job demands (for example, time pressure and high work load), low social support, and low decision-making authority.[1,2]

Signs of severe depression include: tearfulness; crying; sleeping too little or too much; difficulty concentrating; difficulty remembering; lack of energy; loss of appetite, or overeating; feelings of hopelessness, worthlessness, and/or helplessness; self-blame; irritability; anger outbursts; social withdrawal; loss of interest in what was previously enjoyed; and thoughts of death and dying.

A depression diagnosis is a serious matter that needs to be treated promptly, perhaps both through "talk therapy" and with medications.

Research reports a rate of depression for corrections staff, and corrections officers in particular, that is much higher than that of the general population.[3,4]

If you are experiencing depressive symptoms, please seek expert help immediately. Do not ignore them, thinking that they will go away, and definitely, do not try to escape them through substance use or other addictive behaviors.

Depression is involved, at least partly, in substance abuse and suicide. It is to these topics that we turn next.

Reflection: What can you do to deal with "the blues" in healthy ways?

[1]Blackmore, E.R., Stansfeld, S.A., Weller, I., Munce, S., Zagorski, B.M., Stewart, D.E. (2007). Major Depressive Episodes and Work Stress: Results From a National Population Survey. *American Journal of Public Health, 97,* 2088–2093.

[2]Melchior, M., Caspi, A., Milne, B.J., Danese, A., Poulton, R., & Moffitt, T.E. (2007). Work stress precipitates depression and anxiety in young, working women and men. *Psychological Medicine, 37,* 1119–1129.

[3]Denhof, M.D., & Spinaris, C.G. (2013). Depression, PTSD, and Comorbidity in United States Corrections Professionals: Impact on Health and Functioning.
http://desertwaters.com/wp-content/uploads/2013/09/Comorbidity_ Study_09-03-131.pdf

[4]Obidoa, C., Reeves, D., Warren, N., Reisine, S., & Cherniack, M. (2011). Depression and Work-Family Conflict among Corrections Officers. *Journal of Occupational and Environmental Medicine, 53,* 1294-1301.

CHAPTER 10
SUBSTANCE ABUSE

In my trainings, I often ask corrections staff what are their most commonly used coping strategies. Consistently, staff mention alcohol use as one of their preferred coping tools. In this chapter I offer some thoughts on this subject.

Alcohol is easy to turn to. It is legal and relatively cheap. It is also part of the "tough guy" image to which corrections staff adhere. Although alcohol is a depressant of the nervous system, at low concentrations it stimulates areas of the brain that produce pleasure. It thus artificially creates a sense of contentment. In addition to simulating good feelings, alcohol "numbs" distressing emotions, such as sadness or worry. Alcohol can help an agitated person fall asleep.

However, at higher amounts, alcohol impairs brain function, such as rational thinking—even up to seventy-two hours following heavy use. Alcohol suppresses activity in parts of the brain involved in planning and rational thought. It reduces inhibitions, and increases the risk of reacting without considering the consequences. And long-term alcohol abuse damages vital organs, such as the liver, brain, and heart.

Given the many adverse consequences of alcohol abuse, it is critical that corrections staff choose to employ healthy ways to deal with distress, such as have been suggested in prior chapters.

If you wonder whether you are abusing alcohol, answer the questions[1] below honestly:

- Do you call in sick after a day/night of heavy drinking?
- Is your alcohol consumption causing conflict between you and your significant others?
- Do you drink to feel relaxed in social settings?
- Do you drink to cheer yourself up or to forget about distressing emotions or thoughts?
- Do you drink to boost your self-confidence?
- Do you have the reputation that you do embarrassing or violent things when drunk?
- Have you ever felt guilt or regret for things you've done while drinking alcohol?
- Have you caused yourself or your family financial hardship due to consequences related to your alcohol consumption?
- Do you find yourself drinking with people or in places you would normally avoid when sober?
- Do you put family or friends in danger while

drinking, such as driving them around while drunk or exposing them to unsafe drinking companions?

- Have you noticed that your desires and plans for the future have faded since you began to drink more?
- Do you crave alcohol at certain times of the day?
- After a day/night of heavy drinking, do you wake up wanting a drink the next day?
- Do you have difficulty staying asleep after a day/night of heavy drinking?
- Has your performance level at work dropped since you started drinking heavily?
- Is your alcohol consumption putting your job in jeopardy?
- Do you drink by yourself, away from people?
- Have you ever had a blackout (loss of memory of events) while drinking?
- Do you binge-drink?
- Once you start drinking alcohol, do you find it hard to stop?
- Has your physician ever treated you for alcohol-related health problems?
- Have you ever had to go to a hospital or other treatment facility due to health concerns that stem from your alcohol consumption?

If you answered YES to any *one* of the questions, you may be abusing alcohol.

If you answered YES to any *two* questions, chances are that you are abusing alcohol.

If you answered YES to three or more, you are definitely abusing or depending upon alcohol to cope. Seek professional help promptly. Your health, your family life, your career, and even your life may depend upon it.

Instead of or in addition to alcohol, staff may abuse other substances, such as illegal drugs or prescription medications. Or they can become dependent on "process" addictions, such as compulsive sexual activities and gambling. Again, **seek professional help promptly.** Treatment approaches and resources abound. All that is required is your willingness to be set free from the bondage of addiction in order to live a truly satisfying life.

Reflection
What can you do to deal with emotional distress effectively, instead of trying to avoid it through substance abuse?

---

[1]The above questions were modified and adapted from a questionnaire used by Johns Hopkins University Hospital.

CHAPTER 11

CORRECTIONS STAFF SUICIDE

If You Are Feeling Suicidal

Dear Correctional Worker:

Lately you've been thinking that life has become too hard, that holding on is not worth the struggle. Seductive thoughts of "ending it all" comfort you—but they also scare you. They seem like like friends offering an alluring way out. But you don't really want to die. You just want the pain to go away.

Having thoughts of killing yourself is not terribly unusual. None of us likes to suffer. We all want pain relief, solutions for our problems. When cornered, we all want "out." But there are many infinitely better ways to deal with pain than suicide.

I don't know what your circumstances are, but perhaps recent losses or failures feel devastating. Perhaps your significant other informed you that the relationship is over. Maybe you crossed a line at work and you're now under investigation. You might have just gotten a DUI. You may be in serious debt due to your gambling. Perhaps you were diagnosed with an illness which, to you, strips you of your quality of life. Perhaps you have a family history of severe depression.

Sorrow, shame, guilt, regret, self-hate, rage, and worry threaten to suck you down into their black hole. Feelings of worthlessness, hopelessness, and helplessness overwhelm you. You keep flying off the handle or you can barely stop crying. Your mind screams at you, "Loser! You messed up BIG this time! It's over! You're done!" Thoughts of death come masquerading as a merciful escape.

A part of you may be feeling a pull toward self-inflicted death. Yet, another part of you wants to live. Perhaps that is why you are reading this now.

*Please hear me. If you see yourself in what I described above, see a medical doctor and behavioral health professional **promptly**, even if that means going to the emergency room. Or call 911. At the very least, call a 24/7 suicide hotline **immediately**, like the National Suicide Prevention Lifeline at 800-273-8255.*

You need help and support NOW. This may involve psychological treatment and/or medications (at least for a season).

You may not like to take medications. Yet, extreme and repeated stress affects brain chemicals and therefore brain functioning, sometimes leading to depression. If your car's battery was out of juice, you would recharge that battery. In similar ways, to recharge and heal, the depressed brain needs assistance, such as through medications and/or "talk" therapy. Why try to tough it out? So if your physician prescribes medication to help with your mood, please take it faithfully, as prescribed. Make that a priority, no matter how you feel. Do not mix alcohol with it! If side effects bother you, let your physician know, so that a different medication can be prescribed. If you have concerns about your treatment and believe you need a second (and even third) professional opinion, get it. Never give up on looking for help.

Now, about your life situation. Look for a psycho-therapist who uses evidence-based approaches, such as cognitive-behavioral therapy, to treat depression. When we're severely depressed, our thinking becomes muddled. A bad situation appears to us like a catastrophe that can't be remedied. We lose hope that anyone will ever love us again, or that we'll ever feel good again. We believe the lie that we can't get our lives back on track. We become convinced that there is no for-giveness for our wrongdoings. We embrace the lie that suicide is the best option.

We need an objective, compassionate and knowledgeable professional to help us find our way out of this darkness. That person can help us see that these thoughts are distortions stemming from highly charged emotions, and possibly from a chemically-depleted brain.

You ARE worth loving. This is based upon your sacred spiritual core and on Who created you. It has nothing to do with who wants to be with you, your finances, or your professional status.

Life-affirming alternatives to suicide abound. Solutions—short-term and long-term—can emerge as you give yourself time to heal. Do your part— get the help you need—and solutions will appear. Hold firmly onto that hope. You'll watch your depression melt away as you gradually apply more effective ways to tackle challenges, take better care of yourself, and quell emotional storms. Getting through this crisis will result in your adding valuable coping tools to your toolbox.

To overcome the darkness, you also need the fuel of love. Look for a community that will accept you "just as you are." This may be a 12-step group, such as Alcoholics Anonymous, a divorce recovery group, a support group for people suffering from a certain illness, or a faith community. Or it may simply be trusted friends and family.

Good can come out of bad. Mistakes can be amended. Forgiveness can be found. Love can come knocking on your door again. Dignity can be restored. Progress can spring from catastrophes. Purpose can grace your path once more. Peace can reign in your heart.

If you don't yet believe that life can get better, I invite you to piggyback on my hope for you. I know it can.

Here are some resources, just one phone call away, 24/7:

- *National Suicide Prevention Lifeline, 800-273-8255, www.suicidepreventionlifeline.org*
- *Safe Call Now, 877-230-6060, https://www.safecallnow.org/*
- *Serve & Protect, 615-373-8000, http://serveprotect.org/*

The last two organizations exclusively serve first responders (including corrections staff) and their families.

Remember: a vital part of you wants to live. Protect your life! It is a precious gift, absolutely worth preserving!

If You Suspect a Coworker or Loved One May Be Suicidal

Most people who are thinking of suicide communicate that, usually indirectly. Their hints may include statements such as, "Soon I won't have to deal with that anymore," "You won't have to put up with me much longer," or "I've found the ultimate solution." Questions, uncharacteristic for the person, about life after death and about spiritual consequences of suicide should raise red flags. "Wrap-up/good-bye" statements by a person, such as, "I want to thank you for having always been good to me," could also be veiled communications of suicidal thinking.

Communication of suicidal thinking may also be revealed through actions. Giving away prized possessions, setting one's affairs in order, suddenly making a will, or getting a friend to promise to take in pets if something happened to them are examples of warning signs.

Suicidal individuals may drop hints to see if people care enough to really listen, decode their hidden messages, and intervene. So asking a person directly about the possibility of suicidal thinking, as suggested below, may bring them some relief, as it provides them with evidence that others "see" them, care, and are willing to reach out to them. Asking someone if they are suicidal in and of itself will not make them suicidal.

Here, briefly, are thoughts on dealing with some-one you suspect is having suicidal thoughts. (Detailed suicide prevention and intervention trainings are offered by organizations such as LivingWorks, https://www.livingworks.net/.) Ultimately, a mental health provider needs to conduct a suicide risk assessment and determine the next steps of action.

When you notice red flags, ask "the" question compassionately, yet directly: "I heard you say _____ OR I noticed you _____. I care about you very much. Has it gotten bad enough that you're thinking of suicide?"

If the person answers "Yes," do not show alarm. People can have thoughts of suicide at difficult junctures in their lives. Instead, ask, "Have you thought of how to kill yourself?" If they reply affirmatively, ask what their contemplated method of suicide is. Then ask, "Do you have the means to carry this out?" If the reply is "Yes," follow with, "Do you at this time intend to kill yourself?"

The risk for suicidal action increases with the number of "Yes" replies, assuming that a person is answering truthfully. Again, a professional needs to conduct a formal risk assessment.

If a friend or loved one indicate that they are suicidal, do not get angry at them. Absolutely do not tell them they are selfish or cowardly, and do not try to "guilt" them or scare them by using religious terminology. Such statements would betray your lack of compassion, and would make the person shut down and feel even more alone than before they spoke with you. Instead, tell them that you cannot even begin to imagine the pain they feel. Here are some next steps:

- Ask them for their reasons for wanting to die, and listen compassionately.
- Empathize with them regarding their reasons for dying, yet gently state that you believe there are better solutions than suicide – even if they cannot think of any at this time.
- Ask them for reasons to keep on living. If they don't mention any, say, "What has helped you stay alive until now?" And/or, "You may be too upset to think about reasons for living right now, but I believe that they exist."
- Ask, "When you think about suicide, do you really want to die or do you want the pain to go away?"
- Ask, "What are other ways for your pain to go away other than suicide?"
- Ask if the person is currently receiving (or has received) mental health help. If so, assist them in contacting their provider immediately.

Do not leave a person who is having thoughts of suicide alone under any circumstances. As soon as possible, seek help for them. Call 911.

You may be concerned about embarrassing your friend or loved one. Don't take chances with their life. Don't keep secrets. Choose life. Explain to the person that you'd rather they be angry at you – and alive, than dead.

If a person has already acted on their suicidal intent (for example, has taken pills), or seems in imminent danger of doing so, call 911, so they can be driven to the emergency room securely in an ambulance.

If a person seems really sad, but told you that they have no plans or intent to kill themselves, do not leave them alone. Do whatever it takes to have them meet with a mental health provider or physician ASAP. Help them make an appointment, and go with them and wait in the waiting room. Get two or three trusted colleagues or relatives to stay with the person around the clock until the emotional crisis blows over. Steer the person away from alcohol. Engage with them in calming activities that they enjoy.

Mortality data[1] indicate that corrections officers are at a high risk for suicide. To prevent more staff suicides, agencies must train staff on dealing with job stress, train supervisors to be positive and supportive leaders, provide abundant Employee Assistance Program services and health benefits, and offer effective support for those exposed to critical incidents at work. Staff under investigation may be particularly at risk, and administrators need to assist them—through EAP, peer supporters, chaplains, or other means.

Public acknowledgment of the emotional fallout of corrections work – coupled with acceptance of the fact that tough people can seek help when they hurt – may help prevention efforts regarding corrections staff suicide.

And because a healthy spiritual life can boost resilience, spirituality is briefly addressed in the next chapter. If you'd rather not read it, go on to our concluding chapter entitled "Moving Forward."

Reflection
What people, pets, pursuits or projects make living worthwhile for you?

---

[1]Violanti, J.M., Robinson, C.F, Shen, R. (2013). Law Enforcement Suicide: A National Analysis. *International Journal of Emergency Mental Health and Human Resilience,, 15,* 289-298.

CHAPTER 12
A SPIRITUAL SOLUTION

As I sat on my balcony overlooking California's Newport Beach, I contemplated my life. At thirty years old, I had experienced career success in both law enforcement and the military. Named the Honor Graduate of the Los Angeles County Sheriff's Academy, I was now a Sergeant with one of the most respected law enforcement agencies in the country, and also a Captain in the U.S. Army Reserve. Yes, I was successful in my career, but I was a failure as a husband and father. I was empty and unfulfilled inside, and somehow I knew there must be more to life.

As the sun set over the Pacific, I recalled my early years as a young Deputy Sheriff when I was consumed with my career. I volunteered for special assignments, made as many arrests as possible, and spent countless hours in court. I sought to be accepted by my peers and went out drinking with them after work, later to develop a dependence on alcohol. In the process of seeking to be "Super-cop," I neglected my wife and children and went through a divorce.

The following day, as I ran along the coast, I passed a church and noticed a young couple coming out. I was drawn to the peace and contentment I could sense in their countenances—a peace I didn't possess. Somehow I knew the peace I sensed in their lives had something to do with the church they had just left.

I was not raised in a family that went to church or talked about God or faith, but I felt there might be answers to my emptiness inside that building with the cross. I fought the urge to go in, thinking, "Church is for weak people, not Sheriff's Sergeants or Army Captains."

But two weeks later, I went to the morning service and heard a message I had never before understood, but that was to change my life for eternity. What I heard were truths I could understand as a career law enforcement officer, and that are sometimes characterized as The Four Spiritual Laws:

1. God loved me and offered a wonderful plan for my life.

2. But I, and all humanity, was sinful and separated from God. Therefore, I could not know and experience God's love and plan for my life.

3. *Jesus Christ was God's only provision for my sin. Through him I could know and experience God's love and plan for my life.*

4. *I must individually accept Jesus Christ as Savior and Lord; then I could know and experience God's love and plan for my life.*

I now understood why career success, possessions, alcohol, or people could not fill my emptiness. The truth of what philosopher Blaise Pascal once said came to mind: "There is a God-shaped vacuum in the heart of every man which cannot be filled by any created thing, but only by God, the Creator, made known through Jesus." My problem was that I had been seeking fulfillment and peace in my life through everything and everyone but the one person who could give it.

A few days later, with the small bits of understanding and faith I had, I spoke to God and somehow knew he was listening. "God, I'm sorry for my sin. I turn from it right now. I thank you for sending Jesus Christ to die on the cross for my sin. Jesus, I ask you to come into my heart and life right now. Be my Lord, Savior, and friend. Help me to follow you all the days of my life. Thank you for forgiving and receiving me right now. Thank you that my sin is forgiven and that I am going to heaven. In Jesus' name I pray. Amen."

After talking to God in that prayer, I knew my life had changed. It felt as though a huge weight had been taken off of my shoulders. The peace I had been looking for through my own efforts, God gave me as a free gift through his grace and love for me. Since then, I've learned the truth of Jesus' words in Matthew 6:33: "Seek first the kingdom of God and his righteousness, and all these things shall be added to you." As I put God first in my life, all the other parts of my life began to fall into place with a sense of meaning and purpose. The emptiness I had attempted to fill with alcohol was now filled with his love and peace.

God is gracious, and his forgiving hand has given me another opportunity at marriage with my beautiful wife, Ruth. God is at the center of our lives individually and together. Over the past twenty-five years Ruth and I have proven that a marriage in corrections work can not only survive, but thrive. I have found that God's plans for my life are much more rewarding and fulfilling than my own. As I have sought to give God first place in my life, I have become a better husband, father, grandfather, and officer. I now see my law enforcement career with new vision, knowing that God has placed me

in this honorable profession for his purpose, to be
a positive influence in society for him.

~ Mike Raneses, retired parole agent,
California Department of Corrections &
Rehabilitation, founding director of
Corrections Staff Fellowship

To learn more about Corrections Staff Fellowship, visit
www.CSFMinistries.org.

Reflection
How can you increase the giving and
receiving of love in your life?

CHAPTER 13
MOVING FORWARD

We have arrived to the last chapter of this booklet on staying well as a corrections professional. Let us now do a quick review and pull it all together.

To support your pursuit of health and wellness, I wrote about increasing your awareness of how work stressors may affect you. I described the construct of Corrections Fatigue, and phases staff go through during the course of their corrections career in relation to it. I suggested ways for you to take care of yourself and your primary relationships, and ways to maintain professional boundaries. I spoke about serious negative consequences of job stressors, such as PTSD, depression, substance abuse, and suicide. And I presented one person's thoughts on spirituality.

Now pick one strategy proposed in this booklet. Practice it several times per week, ideally daily. Start with a behavior that comes naturally to you. After it becomes part of your life, select a more challenging strategy. Create positive changes in your life through consistent practice.

Here are a few reminders:

- Give yourself permission to be HUMAN. You DO have feelings. You CAN be affected by highly stressful circumstances.
- Identify negative effects of the job on you, and, indirectly, on your loved ones.
- Then think about solutions – what YOU can do to help undo these negative effects and improve your quality of life.
- Process/work through the impact of highly-stressful work events.
- Regularly tend to your physical, psychological, and spiritual needs.
- Nurture and protect your significant relationships.
- Educate significant others about your corrections work.
- Balance the demands of work and home.
- Pursue worthwhile and enjoyable activities outside of work.
- Give out what you'd like to get back.
- Build healthy and supportive relationships with coworkers.
- Seek to develop/improve as a person as a result of work challenges.
- Ask yourself what success is to you; then pursue what to you is a successful life.

In closing, I thank you for choosing to work in corrections. Very few people outside of corrections comprehend the challenges faced by the corrections workforce. Even fewer appreciate the complex skills required to do your job.

Let's keep moving forward together, pursuing both the safety and the sanity/well-being of the corrections workforce! May you embrace health-affirming values and skills. And may you enjoy a sense of fulfillment and healthy pride as you serve in the public safety arena. You, your loved ones, and the profession deserve it.

Reflection
In what ways have I grown/matured as a person due to working in corrections?

OTHER BOOKS
PUBLISHED BY DESERT WATERS

All books can be purchased at http://desertwaters.com.
Bulk discounts begin at purchases larger than 100
copies of each book.

**"More on Staying Well: More
Strategies for Corrections Staff"**
by Caterina Spinaris, Ph.D.
112 pages, $6.49 plus S&H

"More on Staying Well: More Strategies for Corrections
Staff" encourages corrections staff to adopt attitudes
and practices that foster wellness, resilience and job fulfillment—both individually and as a workforce culture.
A broad array of topics is covered, including switching
between the mindsets of work and home life, the re-
laxation response, emotional regulation, sleep, positive
habits, post-traumatic growth, caring relationships,
professional boundaries, trustworthiness, validation,
empathy, and positive meaning.

"This is a much needed resource for corrections professionals. In a job filled with pressures and demands, this
can prove to be a valuable asset to both a personal stress
reduction program and in a training venue. It is apparent that Dr. Spinaris is very familiar with the stress of
corrections and deserves praise for writing a great work.
As a correctional trainer and author, I highly recommend this for all who work in corrections."

~ Gary F. Cornelius, Deputy sheriff (Retired),
Corrections author and trainer, adjunct faculty
George Mason University

"It is well known that stress is pervasive in corrections. If you have 25 minutes or 25 years in the mentally and emotionally challenging vocation of corrections, you know that this is true. The million-dollar question is: "How does one deal with it?" Dr. Spinaris answers this question in a rich variety of ways. I see great utility in how the great ideas are arranged: each section prompts the reader to apply the tactic to themselves. This is crucial reading for those who wish to thrive while in corrections. Those who are retired from corrections can also benefit from the wisdom. Pick it up, corrections colleagues. Your overall health is worth it."

~ Joe Bouchard, Author, trainer, corrections librarian (Retired)

"When Home Becomes a Housing Unit"
by William Young
112 pages, $6.99 plus S&H

"When Home Becomes a Housing Unit" is written by a seasoned corrections officer with the intention of helping corrections staff and their family members understand how work can invade their home life, and how simple constructive behaviors can counteract these negative effects. The overall desired outcome from reading this book is positive life change for corrections workers, and increased two-way appreciation and compassion— of staff for their family, and of family members for their corrections employee loved one.

"Correctional officers toil in virtual anonymity. They are underappreciated, unheralded, and unrecognized for the critically vital role they play as part of the criminal justice continuum. They work in a potentially perilous environment with some of society's most dangerous offenders. The stress endured by these modern day centurions takes an emotional toll. That stress, too, has been anonymous until now. With this work, William Young, a veteran correctional officer, provides intimate anecdotes of the personal struggles that arise from long hours inside unpredictable inmate housing units or bouts of sheer terror that can materialize in a moment's notice. The unique aspect of this work is that not only does Officer Young open the portal to his soul, but he extends an empathetic hand to those who suffer the same or similar fate. He offers encouragement and support to the brave men and women, trained to suppress their emotions, who are tasked with keeping our community safe. Moreover, he lets it be known that there is no shame in asking for help with an emotional burden that is shared by so many working one of the toughest beats in America—jails. I applaud this work and look for more to come."

~ *Mark Foxall, Ph.D., CJM, Director of Corrections (Retired)*

"A stark collision of the complicated and dangerous world of being a corrections officer, while surviving in a world with people who have no idea what goes on behind the walls of a correctional facility. No matter the profession we choose, life creates conflicts between our personal and professional worlds. As Corporal Young vividly describes, these conflicts are heightened by the very nature of the corrections profession. Lengthy shift work, staff turnover, and long-term mental and physical concerns have sadly become part and parcel to this profession. All is not lost though. The challenges that thousands of correctional officers experience on a daily basis can be addressed by taking the first big step: acknowledging the problems. Corporal Young's words shine a welcome and desperately needed light onto our profession. This book is a wakeup call for every new and tenured correctional officer, and a mandate to all supervisors and leaders to finally address the underlying physical and mental impact this profession has on our brave men and women who step up each day to protect their communities."

~ Commander Shawn Laughlin CJM MCJ,
Broomfield Police Detention and Training Center

"Passing It Along: Wisdom from Corrections Staff," Volume 1
96 pages, $5.49 plus S&H

A collection of articles, edited by Caterina Spinaris, Ph.D., on emotional health and wellness by seasoned corrections professionals.

The purpose of this book is to present a compilation of basic principles and tips that contribute to the health of individual corrections professionals, and the health of corrections workplace cultures. The articles in this volume, all written by seasoned corrections staff, address some of the pertinent issues that impact corrections professionals and their families, and offer suggestions for ways to have a successful and satisfying career–and also a good home life.

"Working in the correctional field can be both rewarding and challenging. We don't always realize the effects that being in such an oftentimes negative environment can have on our personality and soul. This booklet provides real life experiences from folks who have walked in your shoes and truly get what you do. I believe the experiences shared here can be of benefit for staff just starting on their correctional journey, and also serve as a reminder for staff who have done their time. Thank you, Desert Waters, for giving the corrections professional a place to feel appreciated and understood!"

~ *Pamela J. Ploughe, Warden (Retired), Colorado Department of Corrections*

"This volume tells the frank truth about 'criminal justice,' and I do not mean the 'PC' version, but the honest, day to day life of loyal, dedicated, selfless professionals who serve and protect our society. It is poignant, candid, broad-brushed, and directed in a meaningful manner to those interested in entering the field of corrections, as well as those presently serving in corrections. The application of this information from the newbie to the seasoned veteran can help promote healthy public safety for the inmates, personnel, and the society at large."

~ *Ron Sands, LMHC, CEAP, Jacksonville Sheriff's Office (Retired)*

"Passing It Along: Wisdom from Corrections Staff," Volume 2
96 pages, $5.49 plus S&H

More articles, edited by Caterina Spinaris, Ph.D., on emotional health and wellness by seasoned corrections professionals.

The wellness and professionalism tips shared by corrections personnel in this second volume of "Passing It Along: Wisdom from Corrections Staff" represent hard-earned correctional experience distilled from a total of 298 years of service in three countries and two continents. They cover a broad range of topics—from dealing with discipline, to women working in corrections, to keeping a healthy balance between work and home life.

"When you attended your correctional academy as a new correctional employee, you were taught your organization's policies, procedures and practices. You graduated, and were told the rest you would learn on the job. You learned that the job is tough, demanding, grueling, and, in many cases, thankless. You often found that you were on your own when you needed to make the right choices and decisions. These articles you are about to read are written by your peers, and could be considered your Master's Degree. If you can learn and apply something from each of these messages, you will emerge at your retirement promoted, effective, successful, happy, proud of your many accomplishments, and realize what a legacy you have left the organization."

~ Gerald M. Gasko, Director of Prisons (Retired), Colorado DOC, LTC. MP. US Army (Retired)

"PASSING IT ALONG: WISDOM FROM COR-
RECTIONS STAFF is a valuable stress management,
personal wellness, and career enhancing resource for
corrections officers and others that work within the correctional system. It provides useful information based
upon the experiences of veteran corrections officers and
specialized mental health professionals. The insights of
its contributors will benefit everyone working within
the field of corrections."

~ Jack A. Digliani, PhD, EdD, Police Psychologist,
"Make it Safe" Police Officer Initiative,
www.jackdigliani.com

"Processing Corrections Work" e-book
by Caterina Spinaris, Ph.D., and
Gregory Morton, M.Sc.
$9.95

This e-book is based on material from Desert Waters'
award-winning course "From Corrections Fatigue to
Fulfillment™". After a review of key sections of the
course, the book presents fillable forms that staff can
review and fill daily or however often they would like to
do so. The text guides staff to process both negative and
positive aspects of their workday, and to explore possible
ways within their control that they can practice to help
improve their work environment. It also reminds them to
implement wellness-boosting strategies both at home and
at work. Multiple-choice and other types of questions are
repeated for each workday.